Smoke a Cigar

A Gentleman's Guide to Cigars, Cigar Smoking and Cigar Accessories

Second Edition

Smoke a Cigar

A Gentleman's Guide to Cigars, Cigar Smoking and Cigar Accessories

Second Edition

J. Matthew Wright

Wright Publications
Key West
2019

Smoke A Cigar: A Gentleman's Guide To Cigars, Cigar Smoking And Cigar Accessories

First Paperback Edition was published in 2010

Second Edition – Paperback
Copyright © 2019 J. Matthew Wright
ISBN-13: 978-1-79907-268-3
ISBN-10: 1-79907-268-1

All rights reserved. No part of this book may be reproduced in any form or by any electronic or mechanical means, including information storage and retrieval systems, without written permission from the author, except in the case of a reviewer, who may quote brief passages in a review. Please send inquiries to: wright.jmatthew@gmail.com.

Any trademarks, service marks, product names and company names cited herein are assumed to be the property of their respective owners, and are used only for reference. There is no implied endorsement if we use one of these terms.

Disclaimer and Terms of Use: No information contained in this book should be considered as physical, health related, financial, tax, or legal advice. Your reliance upon information and content obtained by you at or through this publication is solely at your own risk. The author assumes no liability or responsibility for damage or injury to you, other persons, or property arising from any use of any product, information, idea, or instruction contained in the content provided to you through this book. Furthermore, the fact that an organization or website is referred to in this work as a citation and/or a potential source of further information does not mean that the Author or the Publisher endorses the information the organization or website may provide or recommendations it may make. Readers should also be aware that Internet websites listed in this work may have changed or disappeared between when this work was written and when it is read.

Eating and sleeping are the only activities that should be allowed to interrupt a man's enjoyment of his cigar.

—**Mark Twain**

Contents

Introduction	1
1: Who Invented the Cigar?	5
2: Categorize Your Cigar	9
3: The Three Layers of a Cigar	11
4: Cigars Internationally	13
5: Old and New Cigars	15
6: Cigars for Beginners	17
7: Smoke Like an Expert	21
8: Selecting a Good Cigar	27
9: What the Ashes of a Cigar Tell You	29
10: Cigar Smoking Etiquette	33
11: Cutting Your Cigar the Right Way	37
12: Lighting a Cigar	39
13: Choosing a Great Ashtray	41
14: So You Want to Blow Smoke Rings?	43
15: Introducing the Humidor	45
16: Aging Your Cigars	47
17: Selecting the Best Humidor for Your Cigars	51
18: Smoking Cigars While on the Road	57

19: Enjoying Cigars and Alcohol	63
20: Making Sure Your Cigar Gift is a Hit	67
21: Buying Genuine Cuban Cigars	71
22: Avoid Being Tricked by Dishonest Dealers	75
23: Solving the Tobacco Beetles Problem	79
24: Smoking Cigars on Special Occasions	83
25: Becoming a Cigar Connoisseur	87
Resources	93
Did You Enjoy This Book?	95
About the Author	97

Introduction

With the exciting renaissance of cigar smoking, every novice cigar smoker needs this game-changing guide. It will bring you quickly up to speed to help you become an instant cigar connoisseur who reaps maximum enjoyment from smoking a cigar.

This book begins with a history of cigars and then goes on to explain the parts of a cigar, the construction of a quality cigar and the differences among various types of cigars. From there, the book delves into the cigar connoisseur's most closely guarded secrets, including:

SMOKE A CIGAR

* How to properly select a cigar so you'll never be disappointed again

* How to correctly cut, light, and burn cigars to optimize flavor and taste

* How to store and age cigars to prevent deterioration and enhance flavor

* How to impress everyone with your classy cigar etiquette

* How to end your search for the Holy Grail and acquire Cuban cigars legally

* How to ensure that your cigar gift for a new smoker is a hit

* How to distinguish a fake Cuban cigar from the real thing

* How to treat infested cigars and salvage your investment

* How to increase your cigar smoking pleasure and telegraph your sophistication by choosing the best cigar accessories, including ashtrays, cutters, lighters and humidors

... and much, much more.

Introduction

The cigar connoisseur knows that sophistication resides in the details, as does the enhancement of smoking pleasure. Written for the beginner cigar smoker, this incisive book cuts to the chase, providing the information you really need to impress your friends and extract every last ounce of pleasure from your cigar smoking experience.

1: Who Invented the Cigar?

The history of cigars is rich and diverse. Almost two hundred years ago, when tobacco was first processed in Spain in a cylindrical form, the public fell in love with it; and cigars spread far and wide all over Europe. Meanwhile, here in America, cigar tobacco had been smoked by natives for centuries.

Tobacco was grown in Mexico and Central America for years before it was discovered by Europeans. When Columbus arrived in the New World, he found out about this product and helped spread the word. While Columbus wasn't personally enthralled with it, his sailors and crew were. They helped fuel the expansion of tobacco by sharing pipes with other sailors, whom they met in their travels around the world. From Spain, it spread to Portugal and later to France, where it got the name that we all know.

No one is sure where the word tobacco comes from. It could be a mangled version of the name of the Caribbean island Tobago. It is believed by some to come from the region of Mexico called Tabasco.

The growing of tobacco in the United States is thought to have started in Virginia, where plantations were first seen in 1612. At the time, tobacco was only smoked in pipes. But in the 19th century, as its popularity grew, it began to be rolled into what we now call cigars. An American Revolutionary War general named Israel Putnam first brought cigars to the U.S. after a trip to Cuba. The one box that he returned to Hartford, Connecticut with, would spur the development of numerous cigar factories.

Who Invented the Cigar?

Meanwhile in Europe, British and French veterans, coming home from the Peninsula War in Spain, were bringing back tobacco. If you were among the aristocrats, you preferred your tobacco in a cigar. From that moment on, cigars would be associated with the rich and those that demanded the best.

2: Categorize Your Cigar

When you decide to join the millions that enjoy cigars, you are faced with numerous choices. First among them is to know what type of cigar you are smoking. The two main categories of cigars are parejos and figurados.

Parejo

When you first see a parejo you will notice the shape. They are long and, for the most part, straight. Parejos are made in three types. Coronas have a rounded head and an open tip. Panatelas will sometimes resemble a larger sized cigarette with their long and thin shape. A Lonsdale parejo is extremely long and thin.

Figurado

Figurado cigars come in three varieties and have a more handmade feel and look, as if someone has just rolled them. The belicoso has a small round head and a large open tip. The perfecto resembles something that you might see in an old movie with its thin middle and tapered edges. The "giant of cigars" is the diademas, which usually measures eight inches or more.

3: The Three Layers of a Cigar

Some people smoke cigars their entire lives and don't even know what cigars consist of. Once you learn what the basic parts of a cigar are, you can make choices that will improve your cigar smoking experience.

Wrapper

A large part of the flavor of your cigar comes from the wrapper. This outermost layer is made from the very best tobacco available. The flavor is also affected by the color of the wrapper, which may be light and clear (claro) or dark and rich (oscuro). This layer of tobacco releases flavor that will blend in with the rest of the tobacco in the cigar.

Binder

The next part of a cigar is the binder or intermediary leaves, which literally keeps the inside of the cigar in place.

Filler

The inside of a cigar is called the filler. The cigar's flavor will also be affected by the type of tobacco used in the filler. Cigars of the highest quality have filler made of long, whole tobacco leaves. If the filler is described as short, it consists of cut up scraps of tobacco and results in a lower quality cigar.

4: Cigars Internationally

In the world of cigars, smokers value Cubans above almost every other type. The flavor of a true Cuban cigar is known worldwide. Many times, a cigar will be sold as a Cuban even though it is not. That is because most smokers don't know how to distinguish a Cuban cigar from the cigars of other countries.

Cigars vary in flavor from one country to another based on the soil and climate of the land in which the tobacco is grown. The flavor is also affected by the type of wrapper and the manner in which the cigar is rolled. The design of the cigar affects flavor as well, as cigars with a thicker diameter have a richer flavor.

SMOKE A CIGAR

Cuban cigars are described by smokers as rich, creamy and smooth. Strong and full-bodied cigars are usually from Nicaragua, Honduras or another country in Central America. If you taste a mild flavor, you are more than likely smoking a cigar from the Caribbean, possibly from Jamaica or the Dominican Republic.

5: Old and New Cigars

When you first begin your cigar smoking experience, you will hear about the age of cigars. Some cigars are described as old cigars and some are described as fresh cigars. In reality, unless you own a tobacco plantation, the odds are that you will never smoke a truly fresh cigar. There's a built-in delay factor before a cigar reaches your hands. It must be harvested, processed, manufactured, shipped and ultimately stored at its final destination – the cigar shop – before you purchase it.

In fact, there is a long tradition of the best cigars being made with aged tobacco. Premium cigars typically use tobacco that has been aged for one year or more to enhance its flavor. Then, after the cigar is rolled, it is further stored in a humidor to preserve it until it is sold and consumed.

Like a fine, aged wine, many experienced smokers prefer an 'old' cigar, meaning one that has been aged for a long period of time. Aged cigars tend to be far more flavorful. With the proper temperature (70 degrees) and humidity (70 percent), a cigar can age as long as desired without drying out. Furthermore, dried out cigars, that were not properly aged to begin with, may sometimes be restored by placing them in a correctly configured humidor.

6: Cigars for Beginners

A new cigar smoker may want to try every type of cigar they find. That may sound like the right thing to do, but it isn't. You should start out slow, with light and mild-flavored cigars. Once you have become accustomed to smoking a cigar, you can gradually move up the ladder of flavors until you reach the stronger flavored smokes. Here are five brands of cigars that are perfect for the new cigar enthusiast.

* Punch Grand Cru Robusto

The name Robusto fits this cigar perfectly. Its filler is made from a blend of fine Honduran tobacco.

SMOKE A CIGAR

To fully enjoy these high quality cigars, it is best to store them in a humidor for a few months before smoking. The experience matches the price at $4.00 per piece.

* Baccarat Luchadores

The Baccarat Luchadores is full and rich. If you are a new smoker, it may be a shock to your taste buds. These smokes are slightly unusual in that it is recommended they not be stored in a traditional cigar humidor. They are better preserved in an ordinary cigar box and are priced at approximately $2.50 per cigar.

* Excalibur No. 5

Sold only by Hoyo de Monterrey, the Excalibur No. 5 is a mild cigar that benefits from a quality humidor. It is reasonably priced at $3.25 per cigar.

Cigars for Beginners

* Arturo Fuente Curly Head

This hand-made cigar from the Dominican Republic is perfect for beginners. It delivers a mild taste for the low price of $2.00 per cigar.

* Flor de Oliva Torpedo

The Oliva family produces this cigar with its slightly sweet mild flavor. Made of tobacco from Nicaragua, it is well known and will only cost around $2.00 per cigar.

Any of these fine cigars will give the beginning cigar smoker a solid start on the path of cigar enjoyment. Their mild flavors will make it easier to transition to full flavored cigars.

7: Smoke Like an Expert

Just because you are a new cigar smoker, that doesn't mean you have to act like one. If you observe the following practices, you will appear to be a person who has been enjoying cigars their entire life, even if you're smoking your very first cigar. Some of these practices are delved into further in later chapters.

How to Hold Your Cigar

You may have seen actors in movies holding cigars between their index and middle fingers, as if they were smoking cigarettes, but that is completely incorrect. Sophisticated cigar smokers hold their cigars between the thumb and index finger. It may take some practice, but you will get used to it.

The Cigar Band

Some smokers prefer to leave the cigar band on while they smoke and some prefer to take it off. If you choose to remove the band, it will be easier to remove it if you begin by smoking the cigar first. The heat loosens the band, which will come off without damaging the wrapper.

Lighting the Cigar

You should light your cigar with a match, preferably a wooden cigar match, as opposed to a lighter. A cigar's taste may be changed by the use of a lighter due to the odors from the lighter fluid. The exception to this is a butane lighter, which utilizes a form of liquid gas. When lighting a cigar, hold it horizontally and slowly allow the tip or foot to be heated by the flame. You should take a few puffs as the cigar begins to heat. Let the entire cigar tip receive some of the flame to create an even burn.

To Inhale or Not to Inhale

The proper way to smoke a cigar is to not inhale the smoke. Unlike a cigarette, a cigar smoker can taste all of the body and richness of a cigar without inhaling it. The risk of nicotine addiction rises steeply, as do other unhealthful factors, when you inhale a cigar. Let me repeat, never inhale.

Take Your Time

The enjoyment of a cigar comes from the slow, gentle smoking of it. Smoking a cigar too fast will not allow you to fully savor its taste. Furthermore, frequent puffs will cause the cigar to burn too fast. It should take about an hour to properly enjoy a large cigar, although a Corona can be consumed in about twenty to thirty minutes.

SMOKE A CIGAR

About the Ash

A high quality cigar will have a long ash at the tip. The ash will fall naturally, so there is no need to smoke continuously to see how long the ash will get. If you smoke too long without removing the ash, the cigar will burn unevenly.

The Partially Smoked Cigar

A cigar will stop burning after you have smoked about half of it. If you wish to continue to smoke it, let the cigar ash fall into the ashtray and relight the cigar in the same manner that you first lit it.

If you prefer to leave the remainder for the following day, be aware that cigars that are more than half-smoked begin to lose their taste in two hours. But if you haven't smoked that much, it is perfectly fine to leave the remainder to smoke the following day.

When you have smoked a cigar almost down to the end, it is proper to just place it into an

Smoke Like An Expert

ashtray to burn out. Smoking a cigar down to the absolute end will give you a horrible aftertaste

If others see you enjoying your cigar after you have learned these tips, they will look upon you as a true cigar connoisseur.

8: Selecting a Good Cigar

As mentioned earlier, the way a cigar is rolled and made affects its taste. For example, a strong cigar will have a large diameter and a high quality wrapper. The color of the wrapper will also indicate the type of taste. Before you purchase a cigar, study its appearance. Just by looking at the shape and wrapper, you will be able to determine how well the cigar was made.

A good cigar will have a wrapper that is even-colored and smooth, indicating a consistent flavor. Make sure to avoid cigars with any discoloration of the wrapper, as it signals an alteration of taste.

SMOKE A CIGAR

The cigar should feel firm to the touch throughout its body. If it is soft, hard or lumpy in certain places, it isn't of the best quality and should be avoided.

A gentle sniff will give further clues to the quality of the tobacco. Make sure your single has a pleasing aroma.

Finally, a good cigar will burn evenly if it has been rolled properly, and the ash that is produced will be firm. Loose ash is a sure sign of an inferior cigar.

Like wine, cigars are judged by flavor and body. A strong tobacco will produce a full-bodied cigar. The flavor will also depend on the quality of the ingredients used. High quality tobacco tastes sweet, salty or bitter and produces a good aroma. A cheap cigar will smell bad.

Knowing the difference between a poorly made and a high quality cigar will keep you from wasting money on something you should not be purchasing.

9: What the Ashes of a Cigar Tell You

There are many ways to see if a cigar, that you have just spent your hard-earned money on, is worthy of your purchase. One of the best ways is to check the quality of the cigar's ashes. A simple but brief inspection of your ashtray can tell you a great deal about the cigar you are smoking. You just have to look for the following signs.

As you are enjoying your cigar, watch how quickly or slowly it burns. A cigar that is not of the highest quality will burn too quickly. It will produce ashes that are not firm. The ashes of a low quality cigar will be light and sometimes messy.

As your cigar burns, watch the color of the ash that it produces. A high quality cigar will be made with the highest quality of tobacco possible. The tobacco leaf will burn and leave an ash that is consistently the same color. If you notice a wide variety in the color of the ash, your cigar is not of the best quality.

When a cigar is made in the best manner and with the highest of standards, it will burn and produce ash completely differently than a cheaper cigar. The tobacco mix will be packed firmly and evenly. This type of cigar will burn evenly and produce a stiff, firm ash. The ash of a high quality cigar will stay firm and complete for at least two inches, and will not break apart easily.

While you shouldn't smoke a cigar completely down to the nub, it is possible to do so with a high quality cigar. Any variation in taste that you

What The Ashes of a Cigar Tell You

ordinarily might encounter will be avoided, as you allow the cigar to burn at its own pace.

10: Cigar Smoking Etiquette

To many people worldwide, the time spent smoking a fine cigar is one of life's great pleasures. Your passion for cigars, however, might not be shared by everyone. While you have the right to partake in cigar smoking if you wish, you need to also take into account the preferences of others.

Many smokers sometimes forget that the smell and smoke that emanates from a cigar may only be enjoyable to them and not to other people in the immediate vicinity. The powerful ingredients in the smoke produced by your cigar may linger on clothing and furniture. If you intend to smoke cigars, take note of your responsibility to others. Make it a priority to be considerate of others while you are enjoying your cigar.

If at all possible, try to move your smoking to an area away from those who may be offended by cigar smoke. A good choice would be a room with proper ventilation, preferably a window or a ventilation system. Cigar smoke does contain toxic chemicals, and you should most definitely avoid closed in areas that will restrict the flow of air. Your best option is the great outdoors, where the smoke has the ability to freely circulate. Just be sure to stay away from those that may object to cigar smoke traveling their way. Children, the elderly and people with health concerns are especially vulnerable to the toxicity of cigar smoke.

In the last few years, many cities and municipalities have enacted laws that restrict smoking both indoors and outdoors. In towns and cities that don't have defined smoking laws, individual businesses have created their own restrictions on

Cigar Smoking Etiquette

smoking in their establishments. If you go out to a restaurant or bar for dinner or a drink, be aware of the smoking policies. There are some places that have smoking and non-smoking sections.

If you intend to enjoy a cigar while out, request that you be seated in a smoking area instead of a non-smoking area. If smoking is permitted throughout an establishment, ask those around you if they would mind if you smoked. Try to seat yourself near a window to allow your smoke to travel away from others. And take care to avoid smoking while others are enjoying their meals. A great meal can be ruined by the unwelcome smell of secondhand smoke.

The safe and conscientious cigar smoker should also be aware of how to handle and dispose of cigar ashes. Cigar ashes can become a fire hazard if not properly disposed of. If you smoke outdoors, take an ashtray with you. You don't want to damage your lawn or your property. And make sure that your ashes stay in the ashtray. The

SMOKE A CIGAR

ashes from a less than high quality cigar are loose and have the potential to fly away easily. These ashes could very well fly into your face or the faces of others.

11: Cutting Your Cigar the Right Way

So you are going to enjoy a cigar. You have purchased the finest one that you can afford and are ready to experience the flavor of your cigar. But have you considered a very important step in smoking a cigar? If you don't properly cut your cigar, you won't experience its full flavor.

As you become more versed in the ways of the cigar connoisseur, you will learn that each person performs this task in their own special manner. By studying some of the most common methods, you can develop a method and style all your own.

SMOKE A CIGAR

The first thing to do is closely examine the head of the cigar. This is commonly known as the closed end or cap of the cigar. In order to smoke your cigar, you must open or "clip" this end. Your inspection should reveal where the cigar is closed. Your goal is to not cut too much off the cap. By clipping further than the end of the cap, you risk opening up the cigar and causing the rich tobacco filler to fall out.

To ensure the finest cut possible, you should invest in a high quality cigar clipper. A fine clipper will leave an even, smooth cut. If you are going to invest in a fine cigar, why ruin it with a cheap clipper? A tobacco or smoke shop will have a wide array of quality clippers in all price ranges and styles.

Now that you are ready to proceed, hold your cigar at eye level and clip it quickly and firmly. The less that you clip from the cigar, the better the result will be. If your initial cut is not enough, clip again until you are content with the result.

12: Lighting a Cigar

You have made your purchase and decided on a comfortable place to enjoy your cigar. You have clipped it properly and are ready to smoke it. But if you don't light it properly, it will not be all that enjoyable. There is a right way and a wrong way to light a cigar. Learning the right way will heighten your enjoyment of cigar smoking.

The instrument that you use to light a cigar is important. Using any lighter other than a butane lighter will negatively affect the taste of the cigar and cause an undesirable aroma. The best instrument of all is a cedar match.

SMOKE A CIGAR

Slowly allow the heat of the flame to caress the foot of the cigar, but don't let the foot touch the flame. Aim for a small black ring to develop around the open end of the cigar.

At this point, take the cigar in your mouth and slowly inhale to draw air into the cigar. As you gently rotate the cigar near the flame, you should draw in slowly and smoothly. This gentle rotation near the flame will allow the cigar to be heated evenly and will produce an even burn.

Now that your cigar is lit, take a moment to inspect how the cigar is burning. Is it an even burn? If it is, you lit your cigar correctly. If your cigar is not burning evenly, don't worry. Just gently blow on the end of the cigar to direct the burn around the foot. A few steady draws will prompt your cigar to burn in an even pattern.

13: Choosing a Great Ashtray

As I am sure you know, cigars are not the same as cigarettes. A cigar requires a particular type of ashtray to accommodate its size. And since cigars produce a larger quantity of ash, the ashtray should be able to handle that as well. The mark of an astute cigar smoker is the caliber of ashtray that he selects to hold his cigar.

But how will you know if you have selected a proper cigar ashtray? Your first clue will be the size of the ashtray. Because cigars are not just one shape, unlike cigarettes, your perfect ashtray must be able to accommodate any size of cigar.

Your personal cigar smoking preferences will

also factor into your choice of an ashtray. If the way that you enjoy your cigars produces a large amount of ash, your ashtray will need to be large enough to hold it. If you like to let your cigar rest, your ashtray should be sturdy enough to keep the cigar in place until you are ready to smoke again. The ashtray should support the cigar without pinching or damaging it. A well-designed cigar ashtray made of metal or heavy glass will easily support one or more cigars and their ashes.

Your search for that perfect cigar ashtray best begins at your local smoke shop. They will have a selection of ashtrays made specifically for the cigar smoker. You could also seek out an antique cigar ashtray. An antique ashtray will allow you to benefit from the experience of discriminating cigar lovers of the past. The Internet, flea markets and antique shops are some of the places you should concentrate your search for the best antique ashtray.

14: So You Want to Blow Smoke Rings?

As your skill and experience in cigar smoking grows, you may desire to perform a feat that is synonymous with cigar smoking. Every new cigar smoker wants to learn how to blow a smoke ring. This ability shows everyone that you are a true cigar enthusiast. There is a lively debate over whether this talent can be taught, or if it is something that people are born with. I believe that, with time and a little patience, anyone can learn to blow a smoke ring.

The main ingredient of a luxurious smoke ring is rich, dense smoke. If you can produce this dense smoke, you can produce a smoke ring. Your first step is to take a long puff and slowly draw some of the cigar's smoke into your mouth. The second step is to briefly hold the smoke in your mouth. Now you are ready for step three. That step is to slightly open your mouth and form a rounded "O" with your lips. Finally, pull your tongue slowly back and gently push the smoke out. Your goal is to push the smoke out of your mouth with your tongue, not just exhale the smoke, as exhaling will not produce a smoke ring.

The best smoke ring will come in a place with calm, still air. The slightest disturbance in the air will not allow the ring to hold its form long enough to be a true smoke ring.

15: Introducing the Humidor

When you purchase a box of fine cigars, you don't want to lose a single one. Each cigar is a handmade work of art and must be protected as such. You are not a true cigar lover if you don't possess a quality cigar humidor. A humidor will keep your cigars in the best condition and prevent them from drying out. The humidor will maintain a steady temperature and humidity to preserve the integrity of your cigars.

A humidor will keep the internal temperature of your cigars in a range of 68 to 70 degrees Fahrenheit. The internal humidity will stay between 70 and 72 %. These ranges are set to keep your cigars from prematurely aging. Remember, your cigars are made from a plant. Like any other plant, they will degrade if not properly cared for. Your humidor will keep your cigar in fine smoking shape.

Every great cigar humidor shares the same characteristics. A humidor is not just a wood box; it is a place to protect your cigar purchases. It should be made from the finest cedar wood. Spanish cedar is preferred by most cigar enthusiasts.

A high quality humidor will have a tight seal that prevents moisture from affecting your cigars. You should also be sure to choose a humidor large enough for your particular brand of cigars.

By taking a few initial steps to research the various types of humidors, you can make the most informed purchase possible. In the next three chapters, we will explore how to use a humidor to age a cigar, how to select the right humidor and how to preserve your cigars while traveling.

16: Aging Your Cigars

Aging a cigar and letting a cigar age are two different things, and an aspiring cigar connoisseur must learn the difference. Cigars are like fine wines in that both continue to develop their flavors with the passage of time. Learning to properly age a cigar is an important skill to master. By aging your own cigars, you can avoid spending the money to acquire vintage cigars, which can be very expensive. With just a little knowledge, you can produce the same result on your own. Here are a few tips on proper cigar aging.

SMOKE A CIGAR

Aging a cigar is just like aging a wine. It takes time, which means you should be prepared to wait for your cigars to age. The total process takes at least a year. The change in the flavors which is achieved by aging comes slowly. The process is easier if you start by choosing a high quality cigar to age. High quality tobacco will only get better with time. A lower quality cigar is not a good choice for aging because tobacco that is of less than the best quality will not improve during the aging process.

A high quality humidor is essential for the cigar enthusiast who intends to age his own cigars. The best humidors will preserve and protect your cigars at the best possible combination of temperature and humidity. That combination is a temperature of 70 degrees Fahrenheit and a humidity level of 70%. If this combination is not exact, the quality of your cigars will degrade instead of improve.

Aging Your Cigars

This stable environment is a must for your cigars, even if you are not aging them. Remember, cigars are made from tobacco and tobacco is a plant. Like any other plant, it will degrade over time if not properly cared for. While a plant will die, a cigar will dry out and possibly split open if not preserved correctly.

If you have selected your cigar humidor correctly, it will be large enough to accommodate your cigars. During the aging process, your cigars need room to "breathe." Your cigars also need a humidor that is constructed of the finest materials available. The choice of many a cigar enthusiast is Spanish cedar. As your cigars age, they will interact with the distinctive aroma and natural oils of the cedar wood. This playful interaction between the tobacco and the wood is like the interaction between a wine and the barrel that it is being aged in.

You can expect any high quality cigars, which are presently too strong for your taste, to develop

SMOKE A CIGAR

a mellower flavor after being aged. With the passage of time, all of your cigars will acquire a new and unique taste.

17: Selecting the Best Humidor for Your Cigars

As a cigar smoker, each cigar that you purchase is an investment – an investment in your own personal enjoyment. And as with any investment, your cigars must be protected in the best possible manner. For cigars, a humidor is what is used to guard your cigars against the elements. The original cigar box is just that, a box. It will not preserve your cigars. Only a humidor will ensure that your cigars have the best possible environment to rest and age until you are ready to enjoy them. The best cigars are improved by the careful aging a high quality humidor provides.

SMOKE A CIGAR

Determine the Purpose for Your Humidor

Because humidors serve different purposes, there are numerous considerations in choosing a cigar humidor. If you intend to enjoy your cigars in the comfort of your home, you may select a humidor that matches your home's decor. If you enjoy a variety of tastes, you will want to select one that is large enough to accommodate a wide array of cigars. If you intend to smoke cigars in your office, you may choose a large, cabinet-style humidor that reflects your status. On the other hand, your office may not have room for a large humidor, or the cigars may only be for a special occasion, in which case a tabletop model will suffice. If you transport your cigars, you'll have to purchase a small humidor suitable for travel. You wouldn't want one that is too large to fit in a suitcase.

Consider How Well It Is Made

After selecting the size of your humidor, you have to look at the quality of the humidors available.

Selecting the Best Humidor for Your Cigars

The very best cigar humidors are made from the finest hardwoods. Lesser woods like plywood won't protect your cigars as well. The wood used should be free of any imperfections. The interior will usually be made from one of two materials – Spanish cedar or Honduran Mahogany. These woods have proven to be the best at both protecting your cigars from decay and allowing them to age properly. However, if you are selecting a humidor to travel with, a metal case may be the best choice. Metal will help protect your cigars from being damaged in transit. When you travel, it is best to treat your cigars as you would valuables and not check them in with your luggage.

Evaluate Its Storage Capability and Equipment

Humidors are specifically made to hold your cigars. That is the reason for purchasing a humidor instead of an ordinary wood box. A high quality humidor will allow you to store different types of cigars without their flavors affecting each other. The interior of the humidor will have a hygrometer and a humidification device. While different humidors have different types of equipment, an analog hygrometer displays the same information as the digital version. The humidification device may vary also. For example, some models may include humidification crystals and others distilled water. This is all to keep the humidity and temperature in the correct balance.

Prepare Your Humidor for Cigars

The first thing you should do after purchasing a humidor is to inspect it to make sure that it has no damage and is intact. The included instructions will show you how to set it up. After setting the hygrometer and humidification devices, let the humidor rest for 48 hours. This will allow the interior to become ready for your cigars. After you secure your cigars in the humidor, place it away

Selecting the Best Humidor for Your Cigars

from heat, cold and direct sunlight. Every few days, open it to allow some fresh air into the humidor.

If you have purchased the best humidor that you can afford, you will not have to worry about the condition of your cigars. They will be protected and preserved for years to come. A high quality humidor will not cost a fortune if you know how to properly select one. Now you do.

18: Smoking Cigars While on the Road

Cigars are delicate and must be treated properly when you travel. If you handle them correctly, they will be protected from potential damage. Your selection of a perfect travel humidor will keep your fine cigars in great shape.

Protect Your Cigars

Your travel humidor should be small enough for you to travel with and sturdy enough to protect your cigars. Your best choice is a model that you can carry with you at all times. Don't trust your prized cigars to the baggage hold of an airplane.

SMOKE A CIGAR

The humidor should have enough room for the number of cigars you intend to take with you. You should also check the humidor's hardware. Can the hinge withstand being opened frequently? Will the interior devices hold if they are shaken in transit? Don't take any chances with the protection of your cigars.

If you only intend to smoke a few cigars while you travel, a cigar case may be your best bet. A cigar case will hold one to four cigars and is compact enough to put in a pocket. Cigar cases come in many shapes and sizes. They also come in different materials. One distinctive case is a leather cigar case. Some leather cases have individual compartments for same-sized cigars, which may also expand length-wise to accommodate longer cigars. Individual compartments keep each cigar from moving around as you move around.

If you prefer to travel with different-sized cigars, an open type case, which is free of individual compartments, will be best for you. However, if you carry too many cigars in a leather case, they may be difficult to hide under your clothing. Certain jacket styles work better when carrying cigars.

If you only want to carry one or two cigars, you could purchase cigar tubes. Tubos cigars are individual cigar humidors. They are made with wood interiors and metal exteriors to protect the integrity of your singles. Cigar tubes are not preferred if you intend to carry more than three or four cigars. It would be too bulky to transport more than four cigar tubes.

Getting Ready for Your Trip

As you can see, traveling with cigars can be a rewarding experience if you prepare correctly before you travel. If you consider each step in the process, you should arrive at your destination with your cigars intact. When you return home, your goal is not to return with any of the cigars that you started with. Why travel with too many cigars, as you only heighten the chance of damaging them. A cigar that you travel with and don't smoke is a cigar that could have been aging nicely in your home humidor.

There are certain brands of cigars that handle the rigors of travel better than others. All of the following brands are great choices for travel: La Gloria Cubana Medaille d'Or No. 3, Partagas Corona, Padron Magnum, Montecristo No. 2, Bolivar Royal Corona and Hoyo de Monterrey Excalibur No. 1.

One Last Tip
Once you have selected cigars from your collection and the correct travel device for your trip, you are all set to go. But if you have just purchased the cigars, load them into your travel case without unwrapping them first. Remove the wrappers only when you are ready to smoke the cigars, as they will help preserve them.

Smoking Cigars While On The Road

Your travel case or humidor will keep your cigars properly protected. They will arrive at your destination in the same condition they were in when you left home. Remember, each of your cigars is important to you. If you can't preserve them, you can't enjoy them. By observing these practices, you will be able to enjoy your cigars just as much on the road as you do at home.

19: Enjoying Cigars and Alcohol

When you think of the rich and famous, you imagine them enjoying the finer things in life. The pairing of cigars and alcohol has always been synonymous with living a life of luxury. Now that you have decided to smoke fine cigars, you should also consider pairing your cigar with a good drink. There are numerous drinks that go well with a high quality cigar. If you will allow me, I will give you some pointers on pairing cigars and alcohol.

Television and movies often show cigar smokers enjoying a strong drink with their cigar. That image is partially based on reality, as many cigar enthusiasts do pair their smokes with whiskey, brandy or rum. The sweetness of the alcohol lends a certain taste to the cigar. However, in recent years, smokers have explored combining a good cigar with beer as many beers have tastes that are complementary to cigars. And since most smokers do enjoy a good beer, this natural pairing should not be ignored.

If you make the effort, you will find that drinking a beer with your favorite cigar can be a rewarding experience. However, if you just started smoking cigars, it may be difficult to match your cigar with a beer; a high quality cigar tends to have a strong, powerful flavor, as do certain beers, canceling each other out. But with more experience with cigars over time and a bit of experimentation, it will become easier. Beers are just like cigars. They have varying tastes due to the different ingredients that are used in their creation.

The average cigar can be successfully paired with a single malt scotch or a barley wine. Of the

Enjoying Cigars and Alcohol

two, barley wine is preferred if your cigar has a spicy flavor. The spicy flavor of the cigar blends well with the fruity flavor nodes of the wine. If you use the same strategy with beer, you can achieve some success. A beer that has a slightly fruity flavor will pair nicely with a spicy cigar and produce a smooth, creamy experience.

Enjoy the process of experimenting with pairing cigars and beer. You probably already have your favorite brands of cigar and beer to test. With a bit of trial and error, you will undoubtedly find the best combination for your tastes.

20: Making Sure Your Cigar Gift is a Hit

Is there a cigar lover in your life? If so, you may be trying to find the perfect cigar or cigar-related gift for them. Though you may not view yourself as a cigar expert, that shouldn't prevent you from selecting a gift they will love. Here are a few basic ways to find that perfect cigar gift.

Cigars are no longer just a privilege of the wealthy; anyone can buy and smoke a great cigar now. Before you start thinking about how you can get your hands on the finest Cuban cigars, you should realize that they are difficult to obtain and very expensive. But there are some great cigars you can purchase that won't cost you a fortune and will still be a treat for the cigar smoker in your life.

If you're going to buy a great cigar gift, the place of purchase can make a big difference. A cigar or smoke shop should be your first and only stop. They have a wide variety of cigars to choose from and an experienced tobacconist to advise you on the finer points of cigars. A reputable smoke shop only carries cigars that consist of 100% tobacco. Many other places, like drugstores and supermarkets, will sell lesser quality cigars. The lower price means that instead of containing 100% tobacco, the cigars will have additives and preservatives. A great cigar doesn't have those ingredients, and you should never make a gift of a cigar that does.

A tobacconist can give you the opportunity to closely inspect a cigar, as most of their cigars will be in humidors instead of in boxes wrapped in plastic. Don't be afraid to ask the tobacconist if

Making Sure Your Cigar Gift Is A Hit

you can touch and smell a cigar. They won't be insulted. In fact, they will respect your attention to detail and quality. When you inspect a cigar, you are looking for clues to how it was made. A fine cigar will be packed tightly and firmly. It should be even throughout. Any lumps or soft spots will indicate that loose tobacco was used instead of whole tobacco leaves. Loose tobacco means that the cigar is not of a high quality.

A high quality cigar has a wrapper with an even color. A cigar wrapped with a low grade of tobacco displays marks and signs of discoloration. If you see those signs, avoid purchasing that particular cigar.

Take a few minutes and hold the cigar up to the light so that you can look into it. The tobacco inside of a cigar should be the same color throughout. If it was rolled properly, you will not see a dramatic variation in its color. You want a cigar that has been rolled properly because it will smoke evenly and cleanly.

SMOKE A CIGAR

Different cigar smokers have different tastes when it comes to smoking. If you are in doubt about your gift recipient's smoking habits, you should purchase a long cigar. Most beginners prefer the milder taste a long cigar provides. But if you know your special person has been smoking for a while, there is a better option. A wider cigar has a rich flavor that an experienced cigar smoker will enjoy more. Your tobacconist will be able to show you many choices and help you make a final decision.

21: Buying Genuine Cuban Cigars

In the world of cigars, the most prized and sought after cigars are the ones made in Cuba. However, because of their cachet, Cuban cigars are difficult to acquire. But that doesn't stop people from attempting to obtain these one-of-a-kind cigars. The truth is, you can find Cuban cigars if you know a few simple tips and tricks.

The economic embargo between Cuba and the United States has given many an unscrupulous person an opportunity to exploit cigar smokers. Often, a person will end up buying cigars that are misrepresented as true Cubans.

Before you can obtain authentic Cuban cigars,

you have to understand the reason why they are so difficult to get a hold of. In 1964, the United States instituted an economic embargo of Cuba. This law prevented cigar smokers from legally importing Cuban cigars to the United States. At that point, the finest cigars in the world became unavailable to most cigar lovers. Getting their hands on just one Cuban cigar became the object of many a cigar lover's desires.

What most people don't realize is that there are ways around this law. If you travel to Cuba, you will have the opportunity to bring back certain items from the island nation. Cigars are included among those items, however, there are restrictions. A visitor is only allowed to return to the U.S. with cigars for their own personal use. Be aware that you will be asked to declare them at customs and that you cannot sell them in the U.S.

The embargo prevents anyone from carrying out transactions involving Cuban cigars within the United States. You are forbidden to buy, sell or

Buying Genuine Cuban Cigars

trade Cuban cigars in any manner. If a person is caught in possession of Cuban cigars and they intend to resell them, they may face a hefty $55,000 fine and/or confiscation of the cigars in question.

The scarcity of these cigars in the United States has led to extreme prices. Just one box can fetch a price ranging from $150 to $500 or more. Be aware that "Cuban" cigars costing less than $150 a box are most likely imitations. The Internet is full of companies claiming to sell "Cuban" cigars at a price too good to be true. If anyone offers you a box of real Cubans and they are as cheap as the cigars you usually smoke, decline their offer. They are trying to take your money.

By now, you are probably wondering, "If purchasing Cuban cigars in the U.S. is illegal, how can I get real Cuban cigars without going to Cuba?" One answer to that question is Canada. Our neighbors to the north legally sell authentic Cuban cigars; a short trip to Canada can fulfill your dreams of smoking a fine Cuban.

SMOKE A CIGAR

Recent changes in the law now allow you to legally bring Cuban cigars back to the U. S. from Canada, or anywhere else in the world they are legally sold, as long as they are solely for your personal use. That said, always make sure to check the current laws for the country you plan to visit.

22: Avoid Being Tricked by Dishonest Dealers

The scarce nature of Cuban cigars makes them a target of cigar enthusiasts and criminals alike. Because so many people desire a chance to enjoy the full, rich flavor of a Cuban, others seek to separate those cigar lovers from their money. They do so by selling fake Cuban cigars. There are many ways to avoid wasting your hard-earned money on an imitation Cuban.

The best way to know that you are purchasing real Cuban cigars is to conduct business with an honest dealer. If you have a reputable tobacconist, rely on them to provide you with true Cuban cigars if they have them available.

Even if you trust your smoke shop or tobacconist completely, there is still a chance they may have been taken in by a scam artist and are unknowingly selling fake Cuban cigars. But if you know what to look for in a true Cuban, you will never be fooled.

The box that contains the cigars is your first clue to their authenticity. Any box holding true Cuban cigars will have a distinctive green and white warranty seal. This seal will appear on the front of the box on the left hand side. The seal should have an unmistakable insignia of a shield and a hat. The right hand corner of the box should contain a large white sticker with the word "Habanos" on it. If that sticker is not on the upper right corner, the box may not contain true Cuban cigars.

The box should be intact and its colors bright and rich. If the box has any imperfections, be wary

Avoid Being Tricked By Dishonest Dealers

of its contents. If the cigars have been damaged, the box will also show signs of damage. Be aware that the green and white warranty seal is also present on boxes of Cohiba, Trinidad and Q'dorsay cigars.

All boxes of Cuban cigars have a unique stamp on the bottom. The word "Habanos" is embedded into every box with a heat stamp. Any other type of stamp (rubber or paper) is a sure sign of imitation Cubans. Real Cuban cigars will also have a factory code stamp on the bottom that lists when the cigars were rolled and where they were rolled. The stamp will be in one of three colors – blue, green or black.

Like any high quality cigar; Cubans have a distinctive, rich aroma. If this full, rich aroma is not present, it is doubtful these cigars are real Cuban cigars.

The cigars in the box should be neatly arranged and in order, every cigar facing in the same direction. Each cigar should be cleanly cut, with all of the caps similar. The cigar bands should be identical. If there is even one cigar out of place, this is not a box of authentic Cuban cigars.

A fine Cuban cigar will have the firm feeling of any high quality cigar. A Cuban will never be made with tobacco that is cheap and loose, so if the cigar has an area that feels different from the rest of it, you can be certain it's a cheap imitation.

23: Solving the Tobacco Beetles Problem

Cigars are made from tobacco, and tobacco is a living plant. Like any other plant, it is susceptible to the ravages of nature. Nature provides a unique threat to your cigars known as Lasioderma Serricorne – the common tobacco beetle. Tobacco beetles like to feed on tobacco, particularly the tobacco in cigars. Any cigar, from the most expensive to the cheapest, is at risk of becoming a meal for tobacco beetles.

Wherever tobacco is grown, the tobacco beetle is not far behind, as its purpose in life is to feed on tobacco leaves. Tobacco beetles prefer the warmer climates of the Caribbean, which is where the world gets a large portion of its tobacco. The female tobacco beetle deposits approximately 100 eggs on the tobacco plant in a "grow bag." When the larvae hatch, the hatchlings feed voraciously, moving around on and boring into the tobacco leaves. It is the active hatchlings that lay waste to tobacco.

Tobacco beetles are tough. When a cigar is manufactured, it goes through an extensive production process. While the process can remove most impurities, tobacco beetles can sometimes find a way to live through this process. Tobacco beetles are also immune to many pesticides that farmers use to fight them.

In the rare instance where tobacco beetles survive extermination, they can be quite a nuisance. If they're not found, they can destroy an entire box of cigars before a smoker realizes what has happened. A sure sign of tobacco beetle infestation are holes in the wrapper of a cigar. Un-

Solving the Tobacco Beetles Problem

checked, these small holes can become large holes.

There are ways to battle the tobacco beetle if it has attacked your cigars. A simple kitchen appliance can aid you in the fight. If you have infested cigars, remove them from your collection immediately. You don't want the infestation to spread. The remaining cigars can be put in a microwave to prevent tobacco beetle larvae from hatching.

Three minutes in the microwave should be enough to kill any potential larvae. Transport them quickly from the microwave to the freezer and leave them there for up to 24 hours. If any larvae survived the microwave, they will be destroyed in the freezer, as freezing cigars is known to kill tobacco beetle larvae. After the 24 hour period, take your cigars and let them thaw until they reach room temperature.

When they return to room temperature, your cigars should now be safe. But be sure to inspect them before smoking or putting them into a hu-

SMOKE A CIGAR

midor. Many people have used this process to eliminate tobacco beetles with great success.

24: Smoking Cigars on Special Occasions

Cigars are like fine wines and gourmet foods. They are fine to have on an ordinary day, but on a special occasion they taste even better.

Many cigar enthusiasts purposely save a fine cigar for out of the ordinary events. They feel that during those uncommon times, the cigar imparts a sweeter, more satisfying taste. In each of our lives there are a lot of special occasions, so maybe you will consider smoking a cigar the next time one of them occurs.

SMOKE A CIGAR

Milestones

The unique events in our lives deserve to be marked in a special way. Don't let that job offer, raise or keynote speech go unnoticed. Reward yourself with a cigar to celebrate your increased wealth, status and recognition.

Gambling

The ability to gamble frees us from the constraints of everyday life. A fine cigar in your hand presents a sophisticated image to others while relaxing you and helping your mind to better concentrate on the game at hand.

Thanksgiving

To Americans, Thanksgiving is one of only a few holidays where we indulge ourselves more than usual. A high quality cigar can be considered the perfect Thanksgiving indulgence. Use the holiday as an excuse to allow yourself a delicious smoke, along with that extra piece of cake or pie.

Smoking Cigars on Special Occasions

Birthdays

Each of us observes a birthday each year. The next time your day comes around, partake of a cigar as a gift to yourself. The passing of another year of life is worthy of celebrating in the most enjoyable way.

Weekends

Sometimes, just making it through the week is a reason for celebration. The ability to use your time as you see fit on the weekend is a great excuse to take a break from life's troubles with a fine cigar.

Every special occasion can be marked by the smoking of a cigar. I have listed just a few of them. But don't overlook the significant moments of everyday life. If you look for it, each new day can present an opportunity to celebrate something special with a cigar.

25: Becoming a Cigar Connoisseur

So you are a cigar smoker. That is a fine thing to be, but are you a true cigar connoisseur? Just because you partake of the occasional cigar, and enjoy the feeling of smoking a fine cigar, that doesn't mean you have become one of the rare breed. The cigar connoisseur is the person who understands all facets of cigar smoking. To reach this status, you have to expand your knowledge and experience regarding the world of cigars. It's not easy for some, but you can reach that level by following these four easy tips.

SMOKE A CIGAR

Learn to Enjoy Change

Change is difficult to handle. Most of us settle on something we like and never gravitate away from it. But the world of cigars is vast and wide; there are many styles, types and flavors of cigars. Each person will have their own personal preferences, but to truly become a cigar connoisseur, you must experience all that the world of cigars has to offer. This willingness to experiment will open your mind and palate. How can you be certain of what you like and don't like if you don't try different varieties? You never know when you might discover a new favorite.

Become an Information Hound

The average cigar smoker knows very little about the cigar they are smoking. This lack of knowledge separates the casual smoker from the diehard cigar enthusiast. We live in a world of instant information. There are so many opportunities to learn about the world of cigars. A whole

Becoming a Cigar Connoisseur

host of Internet websites offer extensive information on cigars and cigar smoking. Every bookstore and library has a section on tobacco and where it comes from. Numerous magazines and periodicals are devoted to cigars. There is no excuse for not learning as much as possible about cigars.

Meet the Tobacconist

Tobacconists and tobacco shops represent a wealth of information about cigars. Everything, from the history of cigars, to cigar trivia, to the latest new flavor and type of cigars, can be learned in a cigar shop. A good tobacconist loves talking about cigars and wants his or her customers to know as much as possible. That knowledge produces a better customer who will purchase more because they can appreciate a quality product when they see it. Your local tobacconist can show you how to select the best cigar and how to properly store and age it. So don't hesitate to ask your tobacconist questions. That is what they are there for, to impart as much of their cigar knowledge as possible. If they didn't love cigars as much as you do, they wouldn't be in the business.

Gather With Other Cigar Lovers

A serious cigar connoisseur belongs to at least one Cigar Club. Cigar Clubs are for those that want to experience as much of the cigar world as is humanly possible. They are places for like-minded individuals to bond over their love of cigars. Cigar Clubs usually have cigar tastings and seminars. They can show you how to pair a fine cigar with a fine liquor. They can introduce you to opportunities that you might not ordinarily have access to. Cigar companies sometimes introduce new cigars to Cigar Clubs to get impressions on a new product from the members. Taking the step to join a Cigar Club shows your seriousness and devotion to being a cigar connoisseur.

Becoming a Cigar Connoisseur

If you follow these tips to broadening your knowledge and experience with cigars, you will become a cigar connoisseur before you know it. The road will be long, but it will be enjoyable. Each new day brings a fresh opportunity to learn or try something new. When you reach your goal of becoming a true cigar connoisseur, it will seem all the more worth it because you will have worked hard to get there; that is, if you call enjoying cigars hard work.

Resources

Cigar lovers will enjoy exploring the following online cigar resources, which offer further information about cigars, cigar smoking and cigar accessories.

Websites

https://www.puff.com/
Excellent source of cigar news with a popular cigar forum.

https://www.cigardiary.com/
A place for your cigar reviews plus information about cigars and health.

https://www.cubancigarwebsite.com/cigar/history
The history of Cuban cigars and tobacco.

https://www.wikihow.com/Prepare-a-Humidor/
Detailed instructions on how to use a humidor.

SMOKE A CIGAR

https://www.tobaccointernational.com/resources/
A compilation of online cigar resources

https://www.jrcigars.com/blending-room/
Interesting mix of information about cigars.

https://www.cigargeeks.com/
Extensive database of cigar reviews, plus an international guide to cigar bars and cigar shops.

Gift Ideas

If you enjoyed *Smoke A Cigar: A Gentleman's Guide to Cigars, Cigar Smoking and Cigar Accessories* by J. Matthew Wright, why not give it as a gift to the cigar lovers in your life. It is available from Amazon.com in two editions: paperback and Kindle. It is also available from BarnesandNoble.com in Nook and paperback editions. Please visit Amazon.com or BarnesandNoble.com now to order this book.

Did You Enjoy This Book?

Dear Reader,

Thank you for reading *Smoke A Cigar: A Gentleman's Guide to Cigars, Cigar Smoking and Cigar Accessories.*

If you would like to help us reach other new cigar smokers with this information, nothing would help more than leaving a brief review on Amazon. It will only take you a minute and we would appreciate it very much.

Thanks again, and wishing you all the best,

J. Matthew Wright

About the Author

J. Matthew Wright has been a cigar enthusiast since his first smoke more than 30 years ago. Since then he became well-known for his blog, The Cigar Muse, which detailed his love of cigars and their inspirational effect on his life. Though no longer blogging, the author continues to share his knowledge and passion for cigars by writing *Smoke a Cigar: A Gentleman's Guide to Cigars, Cigar Smoking and Cigar Accessories* and other books.